The Great Australian Property Heist

How Australian politicians and policymakers are destroying the future

by
Larry Flanagan

I0449810

THE DEVILFISH IN EGYPTIAN WATERS.

American cartoon 'The Devilfish in Egyptian waters' showing England grabbing land on every continent, 1882.

Similarly today, the British Banking Empire's policymaking establishment in Australia gratuitously seizes mortgages and imposes debt to destroy the productive capacity of the Australian economy.

ii

Cover image: Cartoon Adapted from edition of 'Road to Serfdom' by Friedrich von Hayek.

ISBN-13: 978-1548930622
ISBN-10: 1548930628
Typeset in Sydney Australia.
Email: larryflanaganbooks@gmail.com

Contents

iv

Preface

The real estate of Australia is being used as a weapon to put a record number of Australians in record debt, while crowding many Australians out of home ownership, while privatising public property, while destroying the potential economic productive capability of the nation, while making Australia a haven for criminal funds from overseas.

The either-or choice between property and human betterment is fundamental to national policy, to the choice of constraints imposed on the financial system, and to the day-to-day month-to-month regulation of the financial system. The choice has been fought over more than once through history. Australia has made a choice, and I think from the title of this book you can guess which one that is.

To put the fork in the road in historical terms, we have:

Life, liberty and property
> *- John Locke and*
> *Voltaire (real name François-Marie Arouet)*

versus

Life, liberty and the pursuit of happiness
> *- Gottfried Leibniz and Alexander Hamilton*

Australia chose the former by the government and public passive accepting policy choices made by the financial establishment – which amount to property before the pursuit of happiness or felicity. We are now reaping the results.

The Australian experience is a great example of how passivity destroys. Through its world-class moral passivity, Australia's political and policy establishment is engaged in mass destruction. However, it is possible to change.

Introduction

A great deal is made about the Australian property bubble, and there is debate about whether the prices are justified. Whether or not there is a bubble in Australia,[1] and whatever arguments are formulated to justify prices – e.g. population is concentrated on the eastern seaboard – the damage has been done.

Whether or not it's a tulip bubble or any other kind of bubble – it's a heist. Mortgaged Australians have had their lives stolen. Home owners without mortgages have had their homes stolen before they got them.

The 'winners' being those who profit by buying and selling 'at the right time' like the lottery winner shipowner Massy in Joseph Conrad's *The End of the Tether* have been introduced to the lottery mindset. Whether one enjoys a windfall from selling stock in an IPO, or from sale of one's property at a greatly elevated price, it's a windfall. 'That's the market.' The unearned windfall that has contributed nothing to the economy, and on the other side of the windfall is the buyer who assumes the burden of decades of debt slavery which affects and restricts their decisions, their cultural and economic contribution, and constrains their thinking.

Banks benefit by lending and receiving interest payments on larger and larger sums, and without actually engaging in the business of banking. Banking is about lending for capital investment in the economically productive future of the country. Australian banks do that only as a minor proportion of their business. For the most part,

---

[1] The Chairman of the Australian Prudential Regulation Authority (APRA) Wayne Byres carefully avoids the 'b word' which is 'bubble' because it would be dangerous to his flock which are the banks: Michael Bennett 'APRA warns banks to review mortgages for dodgy details' *The Australian* 21 October 2016. Source: http://www.theaustralian.com.au/business/financial-services/apra-warns-banks-to-review-mortgages-for-dodgy-details/news-story/d32bf5094725b992a77e167dcdc56385

they just lend for residential housing which is a consumption item, not an economically productive capital item. In one sense, they are glorified building societies but actually are much more nefarious than building societies. Moreover, they earn much greater interest than they should because value ascribed to the underlying asset is excessive. So banks get an easy life, as do the politicians and policymakers which protect them.

The pursuit of home ownership has largely destroyed the economic contribution of Australians over the last 30 years. Politicians will point to statistics to contradict this assertion. However, there are plenty more statistics and principles to support it.

This is a heist that Australia's culture is ready for. Just as the Indian rajas through their lust for silver allowed the British to play them off against one another, similar the Australian culture's lust for property and adulation of property rights prepared them for – and made them complicit in the heist, even though they are the ones who are fleeced.

Larry Flanagan, Sydney Australia
1 February 2017

1. Have versus have-nots

Australian politicians, and policymaking and regulatory establishment, are worse than a waste of space - they are actively destroying Australia's future. Millenials are known to say "I hate all generation X and boomers" – even those who don't own their own home. However – blessed are the peace makers. There is a lot to make peace about.

Adapted from Fitzsimmons cartoon.[2]

Australians might complain about Islam taking over, quite apart from terrorism, but the policy framework is barely Christian. The policy establishment promotes and actively participates in the situation, while saying everything is fine. Policymakers and politicians pat themselves on the back for doing a great job.

---

[2] Obtained from article by Steven Hsieh at:
http://clearingthefogradio.org/rich-killing-us-nukes-endangering-us-drones-killing-us-and-dhs-spying-on-us/

2. Real estate 'investment' – a parasitical culture

The science of economy is the science of increasing human power or ability to do work. Normally, more advanced engineering and scientific discovery – and enabling those endeavours – are at the core of what economics is. Unfortunately, buying or building a house for someone else to live in is seen as an option for economic endeavour. Yet a home – which is a necessity of life – allows people to shelter from the elements and do work, but is not directly connected to increasing human power or ability to do work, and has little to do with more advanced engineering or scientific discovery. It would be the same if 40 per cent of bank lending were for the growing of wheat. We would be awash in wheat, which is an excellent source of protein and fibre for engineers and scientists, but we would have little for the well-fed engineers and scientists to do because no resource is being allocated to those capital investment projects which ultimately increase human power or ability to do work.

The very idea that real estate is an investment belies the mindset that economics is about extraction from the necessities of life.

Since there are few other games in town, many reach the conclusion that the only way to get ahead is to become a parasite yourself. They act accordingly.

Of course, negative gearing fosters that attitude and rewards it, by exempting people from tax on interest costs for borrowing to buy this one particular asset class. This benefits the usurers, and the speculators who buy the 'investment' property.

Scaremongering on the effect of removing negative gearing is a kind of rigging of the market, because it guarantees future financial flows into real estate which would not be profitable without reduced tax. There also is the psychological lift given to real estate in Australia. The real estate lobby groups work with the real estate owning politicians, along with developers with interests intertwined with real estate agents. Developers lobby and influence social co-minglers at the Australian Prudential Regulation Authority (APRA) who set financial policy to favour property developers and banks.[3]

To be innovate is to renovate, and sell for someone else to live in, or do a reno on your own home to increase its resale value. Housing is a necessity of life but, ultimately, a consumption item like wheat. Hoarding a necessity for price appreciation or rent on standard view is a kind of parasitism.

Sadly a good proportion of Federal Australian Members of Parliament (MPs) and Senators have adopted this themselves.[4] One of them even wrote out to their colleague MPs informing them that they should not respond to surveys asking about MPs' property holdings. Arguably, MPs that hold investment property are not fit to engage in policy debates and should be required to resign.

International buyers of real estate benefit in the short-term by buying real estate, which adds to the phenomenon of people –

---

[3] For more on how social co-mingling drives property prices and promotes rentier-usury extraction from people see Murray, C. and Frijters, P. *Game of Mates: How Favours Bleed the Nation* Cameron Murray 2017.

[4] 'Houses of Parliament: Politicians own an estimated $370m of property' 20 April 2017 *Sydney Morning Herald* Adam Gartrell and Tom McIlroy Source: http://www.smh.com.au/federal-politics/political-news/houses-of-parliament-politicians-own-an-estimated-370m-of-property-20170420-gvp2g5.html

especially young families – being unable to afford to buy a home. Many countries impose constraints on foreign ownership, but not Australia – because politicians and policymakers want to promote inflating property prices.

Many media articles have been written condemning negative gearing yet the political class do nothing. Indeed the Australian public are probably not convinced it is right to remove negative gearing, because Australian culture as it stands today puts property rights on a pedestal above human values. From education to academia to think tanks to politics to media, the Australian zeitgeist considers economics and national policy to be founded on accounting and money, rather than increasing the human power or the ability to do work of Australia as a nation.

Ultimately, national productive capacity drives accounting and requirement for debt, not the other way around. The result is that as a nation we are not very good at balancing the books nor are we particularly productive.

The 'innovation' push of Prime Minister Turnbull's regime is merely a scam, to use digital gadgets or cut corners, rather than having anything to with the science of economy.

3. Black money in Australian real estate

Real estate is exempt from Anti-Money Launder and Counter Terrorism Financing (AML-CTF) regulations. As a result, black money pours into Australian real estate and inflates prices. The Australian government and public know that money laundering through real estate is ongoing.[5],[6]

Restricting the flow of black money into Australian real estate would arrest price increases in real estate. Demonetization in India in late 2016 removed large sums of black money from circulation which had a short-term effect on the rate of increase in real estate prices. It is also is accepted that real estate in India now can build on a more solid, transparent – not to mention less criminal – foundation.

The Financial Action Task Force (FATF) said in the Executive Summary of an April 2015 report that Australia:[7]

---

[5] Source: http://www.austrac.gov.au/money-laundering-through-real-estate
[6] 'ANZ [bank]'s head of financial crime, Guy Boyd, said the lack of regulation makes Australia an attractive target for money launderers. "I think Australian real estate is obviously an attractive destination for capital, both legitimate and illegitimate," he said. "I wouldn't know if I would call it a haven but certainly it is a place of choice for illegitimate money. … There's been probably a lack of political will and that's probably been driven by some very vocal opposition from those industry sectors."' Source: http://www.abc.net.au/news/2017-07-13/should-australias-anti-money-laundering-laws-be-extended/8703354
[7] *Anti-money laundering and counter-terrorist financing measures Australia: Mutual Evaluation Report* April 2015 Financial Action Task Force (FATF) Source: http://www.fatf-gafi.org/media/fatf/documents/reports/mer4/Mutual-Evaluation-Report-Australia-2015.pdf

... is seen as an attractive destination for foreign proceeds [of crime], particularly corruption-related proceeds flowing into real estate, from the Asia-Pacific region. (page 7)

... remains at significant risk of an inflow of illicit funds from persons in foreign countries who find Australia a suitable place to hold and invest funds, including in real estate. (page 10)

Australian policymakers have refused to include real estate in AML-CTF constraints.[8] A review of AML-CTF requirements was tabled in parliament on 29 April 2016.[9]

The recommendations for real estate were soft touch on expectations for action from the government, saying that the government should:

(a) in consultation with industry develop options for 'regulating lawyers, conveyancers, accountants, high-value dealers, real estate agents and trust and company service providers under the AML/CTF Act', and

(b) conduct a cost-benefit analysis of those options.[10] Clearly with lawyers and real estate agents so involved, such a process was guaranteed to produce nothing.

It appears that either (a) produced zero options because real estate agents, lawyers and the government did not want any options, and/or (b) the cost-benefit analysis was not conducted publicly and real estate agents, lawyers and the government decided that the cost of preventing criminal money flowing into real estate – i.e. less rapidly rising real estate prices and

---

[8] Source: http://www.smh.com.au/business/the-neverending-money-laundering-review-20160306-gnbse0.html

[9] Source: https://www.ag.gov.au/Consultations/Pages/StatReviewAntiMoneyLaunderingCounterTerrorismFinActCth2006.aspx

[10] See page 151

reduced business from criminals for real estate agents and lawyers – exceed the benefit.

The government ran a four-week consultation on changes to the regulations from 24 April to 22 May 2017, but the changes do not include any proposed regulations for real estate agents or lawyers.[11] Normally, the purpose of a government consultation is to allow the government to conduct a cost-benefit analysis on the cost to industry of the proposed regulations versus the benefit to Australia.

Banks do not keep reportable or structured records on the property purchased with the loaned funds. This clouds the audit trail on where vast sums of mortgage loans are spent. As banks do not keep up-to-date records on their customers' addresses – in breach of the AML-CTF rules[12] – the opportunities for money laundering through real estate are further enhanced.

---

[11] Source:
http://www.mondaq.com/australia/x/593754/Money+Laundering/Consultation+On+Proposed+Amendments+To+AMLCTF+Rules

[12] See the AML-CTF rules paragraph 4.2.3 here:
https://www.legislation.gov.au/Details/F2017C00526

4. 'New estates' – privatisation without discussion and 'conjuring' value

UrbanNSW conjures prime real estate out of thin air. By creating no value and a façade of advanced lifestyles – which essentially is broadband internet – the NSW government and its advisors are part of a movement to create a façade of value.

Conjuring tricks to create the appearance of value are underway around the world,[13] and the world's best conjurers are at work in Australia. Conjuring tricks in New South Wales Australia over 2014 to 2017 include:[14]

1. The Ponds (Stages 1-4)
2. Rouse Hill
3. Thornton
4. Caddens
5. Bunya
6. Riverstone
7. Schofields Terrace
8. Highcrest
9. Edmondson Park
10. Oran Park Town
11. Claymore
12. One Minto
13. Airds/Bradbury
14. UWS Campbelltown (Macarthur)
15. Spring Farm (East Village)
16. Potts Hill
17. Renwick
18. Menangle Park
19. Elizabeth Hills
20. Fishermans Bay
21. Sanctuary
22. Vantage
23. Herring Road
24. North Ryde Station Precinct
25. Wentworth Point
26. North West Urban Renewal
27. Parramatta North Urban Renewal
28. Parramatta Road Urban Renewal
29. The Bays Urban Renewal Program
30. Central to Eveleigh Urban Renewal and Transport Program
31. Green Square Town Centre
32. Newcastle Urban Renewal and Transport Program

---

[13] Hudson Yards, New York 'Conjuring prime real estate out of thin air' Slide 10 http://www.sbe16sydney.be.unsw.edu.au/DavidPPT.pdf

[14] Slide 9 http://www.urbangrowth.nsw.gov.au/assets/Publications/2014-UGNSW-AnnualReport.pdf

When new estates are opened up, state and territory governments milk the population by elevating lands prices. A minimum of facilities are added, and marketing campaigns added on top, to justify the extortionate indebtedness that the governments cause. This is known as balancing the budget using debt slavery.

Governments are happy to sell assets at extortionate prices without any commitment to maintaining the value. The obvious example is taxi licences. Having sold taxi licences for hundreds of thousands of dollars, Australian governments are happy to allow Uber to operate to white-ant the value of taxi licences sold.

Housing commission estates are knocked down with spurious arguments about 'social problems'. Then the land is sold as a new suburb at extortionate prices. This was done in Claymore, Airds and Minto. The low-income or no-income public housing residents were moved to streets of mortgagors and renters where former housing commission residents are ostracised. Former housing commission residents do not 'pick up the habits' of mortgagors and renters but, rather, cause resentment amongst their neighbours and further withdraw from the community. The state government does not care, nor do the banks, because the housing commission suburbs were released as 'new estates' for debt slaves to live in.

According to the Landcom website at the time of writing, land currently is available at:

- Vantage – Corlette
- Oran Park Town
- Macarthur Heights
- Renwick – Mittagong
- Newbrook – Airds
- Hillcroft – Claymore

Defence Housing Australia has managed to generate enormous returns and we need to ask whether such returns are real.

There were 22 projects on the Urban Growth NSW website at the time of writing.[15]

Consider the Macarthur Heights project as an example. These 'back of envelope' calculations indicate the scale of financial chicanery, or usury, underway:

Macarthur Heights $300m end 'value', from $150m investment in 900 lots and residential dwellings, 2460 new residents; average investment $167k per lot, cost is $333k per lot. Where is the $150m balance? It is in mortgages – pure 'profit' on the heads of people. Not only profit for the state government. Double the $300m in mortgages over the life of the loans, which is $600m for banks. So for $150m 'investment', home mortgagors give the government $150m back plus another $150m, and then give banks $600m, for a total of $900m.

Divide that by 900. Each of the 900 lots comes at a price of $1.3m. If you argue that each of the lots can be sold at a higher price so that the individual mortgagor does not end up actually paying the $1.3m then you have a buyer who will end up paying more than $1.3m, and moreover you also have a ponzi scheme rather than legitimate economic policy.

Not factored into the above is that there is minimal transport or jobs where these estates are located. So the cost of travel time and lack of cultural facilities is not taken into account. If at least one working person per home travels at least 30 minutes longer each way due to the lack of investment in modern transport, then we have 235 hours per year per working resident, or 31 working days of 7.6 hours per day per year. Over 30 years this is 3.9 years' worth of working time.

Even if there is just one working person per household, then the government has created a loss of 3552 person years. At a relatively modest $100,000 of economic contribution per person per year, this comes to another $350m. Person years in commuting are years not spent with other people such as spouse and children which we cannot put a price on.

---

[15] Source: http://www.urbangrowth.nsw.gov.au/projects

Higher property and real estate prices of course translate to higher stamp duty revenue for state governments, and higher council rates for local governments. However, both state and local governments are cutting back on their services. This indicates that the real estate centric economy is not producing because there is no net return from the government-led fleecing schemes.

If we multiply the above figures, we get a bigger picture view for NSW alone:

- 3552 person years wasted by lack of transport infrastructure investment: 78,144 years;
- $26.4b in debt with concomitant benefit to the financial sector; and
- $3.3b in windfall profit to the state government

One arguably could go further and say 900 lots per project × 22 projects × 30 years career of one person per lot, for a total of 59,400 years are wasted because the entirety of people's careers are spent repaying debt and for no other economic motive.

Selling off the land as estates is privatisation. The land no longer is available for government or public use. There was no debate or discussion about this privatisation. Asking the buyers of the property to pay for connection of infrastructure is a kind of 'user pays' for infrastructure *en masse* – again, without public debate or discussion. This sounds like a policy and procedure advised by private investment bankers.

The links between government infrastructure departments and investment banking firms are strong. There are officers who serve in senior, even leadership capacities, both in government infrastructure agencies and investment banks simultaneously.

One wonders which investment bankers and advisers prompted governments to adopt this strategy. It is a win-win for banks and government, but a bigger win for banks.

5. Banks in their element

Today, usury is normal.[16] 'Commercial opportunity' is synonymous with the right to extract rent in the form of whatever interest charge one can get away with.[17] It is not the opportunity to add value, nor barely related to business as such, but is extraction while doing little or nothing except monitor workers. At the heart of this orientation is a slave owner mentality. Yet Australians agree with it, and do not think through to the consequences even while being appalled at the outcomes in their lives and in the country more widely. It is unsurprising that banks comprise 9 per cent of GDP.[18] Again, this is considered appalling, yet the cultural orientation that produced the status quo is well-entrenched.

---

[16] Usury is extracting work, assets or other value from people through financial manipulation. Historically, usury has meant lending at exorbitantly high interest rates, which banks do with credit cards and personal loans, but banks and policymakers are adept at usury even when interest rates are low.

[17] For example, this is the central premise of *A Framework for the Valuation of Loss of a Commercial Opportunity* PhD thesis, University of Sydney February 2016. It is not surprising that the epigram is by Oliver Wendell Holmes, promotor of British cultural pessimism and the might-is-right in the US policy and judicial circles, and the case study is 'Valuation of loss of a lending opportunity'. Source: https://ses.library.usyd.edu.au/bitstream/2123/15542/2/2016_Benjamin%20_Curtin_thesis.pdf

[18] 'The financial services and insurance sector, one of 19 sectors whose "gross value add" the ABS tracks every three months, had increased to 9 per cent of GDP for the first time ever, more than that of retail and wholesale trade combined, according to last week's national accounts.' From 'How the big banks are getting bigger' *The Australian* 14 June 2017 by Adam Creighton. Source: http://www.bfcsa.com.au/index.php/entry/bfcsa-how-the-big-banks-are-getting-bigger-grave-concerns-re-share-of-economy

Banks milk the market and affect their own prudential safety, while misdirecting resources. It is easy money for them. They know that they will enjoy bail in and/or bailout for not thinking, and for cranking the handle.

Chart 1: Australian authorised deposit-taking institutions (ADIs) loans by category ($AUD billions)[19],[20]

	As at 31 Mar 2016	As at 30 Jun 2016	As at 30 Sep 2016	As at 31 Dec 2016	As at 31 Mar 2017
Amount ($AUD billions):					
Total loans	2,907	2,978	3,010	3,064	3,055
Residential real estate	1,754	1,801	1,826	1,860	1,866
Commercial real estate	254	257	261	260	264
Other than real estate	900	921	923	943	925
Proportion of total loans:					
Residential real estate	60%	60%	61%	61%	61%
Commercial real estate	9%	9%	9%	8%	9%
Other than real estate	31%	31%	31%	31%	30%

[19] Source of total loans and housing loans statistics: *Quarterly Authorised Deposit-taking Institution Performance March 2017* http://www.apra.gov.au/adi/Publications/Pages/adi-quarterly-performance-statistics

[20] Source of commercial property statistics: *Quarterly ADI Property Exposures statistics March 2017* http://www.apra.gov.au/adi/Publications/Pages/Quarterly-ADI-Property-Exposures-statistics.aspx

Financial sector regulatory policy starves other economic sectors of credit while transmitting excess credit to residential housing, as chart 1 shows.

Chart 2 presents the proportion of total loans information from chart 1 on proportion of total loans graphically.

Chart 2: Australian authorised deposit-taking institutions (ADIs) loans for housing and commercial real estate as a proportion of total loans[21]

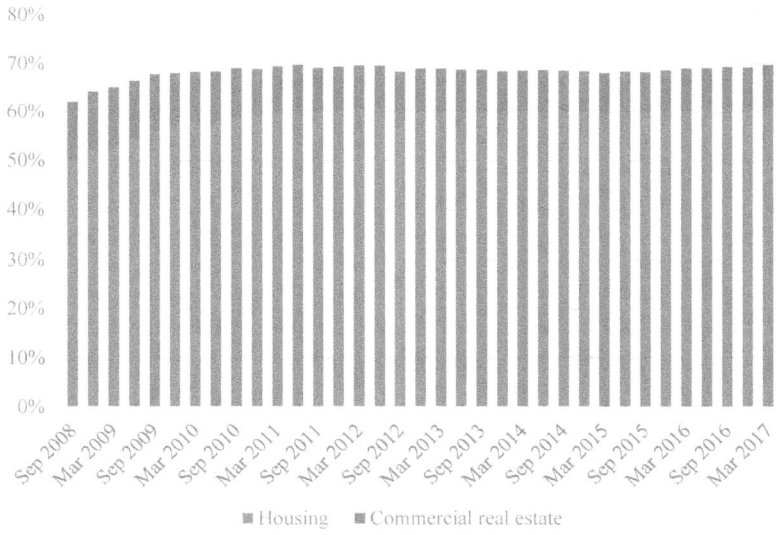

Compare the proportion of banks loans for residential real estate extended by Australian banks with American banks, chart 3.

---

[21] See footnotes on previous page.

Chart 3: Bank lending in USA by category of loan in USA,[22] compared with Australia.

	Loans in $USD in USD as at 31 Mar 2017	Proportion of total loans in USA as at 31 Mar 2017	Proportion for same category of loans in Australia as at 31 Mar 2017
Total loans	9,144 billion		
Residential real estate	2,147 billion	23%	61%
Commercial real estate including development	2,004 billion	22%	9%
Total real estate loans	4,151 billion	45%	70%
Commercial and industrial loans	2,087 billion	23%	APRA does not report

Banks in Australia are not performing the function for which they exist. The role of credit is to marshal effort to bring the future into the present to uplift the national economy with greater productive capacity. The above figures on the proportion of credit in residential real estate indicate that banks have no inclination to enhance the productive capacity of the nation and need to be forced if they are to do so.

The government must step in and either nationalise the banks, or at least set minimum levels of lending for productive capital investment because banks will not perform their function if left to their own commercial decision making criteria.

---

[22] Source: https://www.federalreserve.gov/releases/h8/current/default.htm

APRA has demonstrated that it does not take an interest in productive capital investment nor even the need for productive capital investment to ensure financial stability. This is natural because APRA sees itself as an extension of the Bank for International Settlements (BIS) which takes an entirely monetarist ideology and therefore does not consider drivers of economic growth.

APRA is a secretive extension of international bodies with contempt for the national interest. APRA is captured by industry leaving little ability to regulate, and what may have remained is emasculated by the BIS ownership over APRA's policymaking and supervisory processes and culture.

APRA should be shut down and its functions taken over not by the Reserve Bank of Australia but by Treasury with direct oversight by Parliament. The business of banking is too important to be left to 'independent' agencies.

6. Systemic control fraud

Banks target home owners for investment loans. The 40-60 per cent of loans being for investment are partially secured against the investment property and partially against the home in which the borrower lives. Many of the borrowers do not have the capacity to repay the loan, and so the bank gains the upper hand and can extend more credit to avoid the customer going into arrears with the ability to pull the pin on the borrower when the bank wishes.[23]

There are thousands of cases of lenders choosing to not verify borrower income, and using the poverty line to impute expenses rather than actual expenses of borrowers. There are hundreds of known cases of lenders modifying the borrower's loan application form (LAF) to bump up the borrower's income and assets in order to make the borrower look eminently creditworthy. The same has been found to be happening in Ireland[24] and Canada[25]. The result is that banks,

---

[23] *Rolling Stone* magazine referred to Goldman Sachs both as a vampire squid and as home snatchers. Source: http://www.rollingstone.com/politics/news/the-great-american-bubble-machine-20100405

[24] 'In 2010, Dublin lawyer Vincent Martin and his colleagues were contacted by a man who was at loggerheads with the Irish Nationwide building society, a local bank. After obtaining the bank's files on his account, the man had discovered the bank, which has since merged with Anglo Irish Bank, had created a new version of him for their credit committee. So they could lend him more money during Ireland's bull market, banking officials had changed the man's occupation, inflated his roughly $39,000 annual salary to $78,000, and forged both his and his employer's signature.' Source: http://www.bfcsa.com.au/index.php/entry/bfcsa-irish-anglo-bank-same-as-australia-tricky-wording-on-lafs-39-000-annual-salary-to-78-000-and-forged-signatures

credit unions, building societies and other lenders have emitted billions of dollars of credit into Australian residential housing even while the borrowers under normal serviceability criteria did not qualify for the loans.

The control fraud scam was executed in the USA, and has been brought to Australia in more refined form. The work of Professor William Black, former US regulator,[26] is available in Australia and has been referred to regulators. Unfortunately, regulators in Australia ignore Black's analysis and turn a blind eye to control fraud by Australian banks and building societies.

---

[25] 'The company [Home Capital Group Inc.] terminated its previous CEO, Martin Reid, in late March, after it landed in hot water with securities regulators for failing to disclose that some mortgage brokers in its network were submitting fraudulent documentation. Since then, Bonita Then, who sat on the company's board, has served as interim CEO.' Source: https://www.theglobeandmail.com/report-on-business/home-capital-names-veteran-of-canadian-mortgage-industry-as-new-ceo/article35662930/

[26] Black, W. *The Best Way to Rob a Bank is to Own One: How Corporate Executives and Politicians Looted the S&L Industry* University of Texas Press 2013. Also see the TED Talk by William Black 'How to rob a bank (from the inside, that is) accessed on 11 July 2017 at https://www.ted.com/talks/william_black_how_to_rob_a_bank_from_t he_inside_that_is/transcript?language=en

7. Plenty of supply

The fraudulent argument is being made that high prices are caused by a shortage of supply, and rather than hyper-demand created by excessive credit and black money. The purpose of the false claims about housing supply is to allow government and regulators to turn a blind eye to systemic control fraud by banks, and to turn a blind eye to the flow of black money into Australian real estate.

There are about 1 million empty homes across Australia, 'At the time of the [2016] census, 11.2% of dwellings were recorded as unoccupied – which worked out at 1,089,165 dwellings across Australia. This was a little higher than the previous census [2011] result of 10.2% or 934,471 dwellings.'[27]

Despite the neverending 'population ponzi' arguments from the Macrobusiness website which have validity as far as depressing wages, or at least wage growth, the housing being built has amply kept up with immigration. Importantly, the growth in housing supply has kept pace with the growth in population.

Writer Rob Burgess has explained the con job.[28],[29]

> So the dwellings are there, but either not on the market or increasingly unaffordable if they are.

---

[27] Source: https://www.corelogic.com.au/news/three-unique-housing-insights-from-the-2016-census

[28] Source: http://thenewdaily.com.au/money/property/2017/04/11/housing-supply-con/

[29] Source: http://thenewdaily.com.au/money/finance-news/2017/06/27/census-housing-supply/

What's maddening about those two problems is that they are caused by politicians, not 'the market' as the pollies always try to pretend.

There are two categories of market participants that have led to this situation.

One is overseas property investors, dominated by buyers from mainland China. They are permitted to buy only new dwellings – a rule that is supposed to stimulate housing supply and put downward pressure on prices.

In reality, there are two major exemptions. They can buy homes for their adult children to live in during periods of study in Australia, and, more recently, to house children as young as six who enrol in Australian primary schools.

But the investors who are leaving properties vacant aren't interested in accessing education. They buy off-the-plan apartments as a store of wealth, much like giant gold bars.

The second class of market participants operating in a decidedly non-free-market way are local investors seeking to minimise tax through negative gearing and profit from the 50 per cent discount that applies to any capital gains they make.

Those investors are subsidised by other taxpayers to outbid would-be owner-occupiers.

LF Economics has explained quantitatively how we know there is plentiful housing supply.[30,31]

---

[30] Source: http://www.lfeconomics.com/reports/the-australian-phantom-housing-shortage/

[31] Source: https://www.lfeconomics.com/analysis/housing-affordability-crisis-house-prices-not-rents/

8. First home owners grants

On 1 July 2000, the Australian Federal government in collaboration with the state and territory government introduced the First Home Owner Grant (FHOG) on 1 July 2000. It was a national scheme funded by the states and territories, and administered under each state's and territory's own legislation. The public purpose was to offset the effect of the goods and services tax (GST) on home ownership.[32]

The rationalisation does not make sense. GST is 10 per cent of goods and services input to the construction of a home. The FHOG was a flat amount, regardless of the value of the home purchased. The FHOG changed over time and was different in different states, even though the GST is the same nationwide.

Consider an example. As a result of GST, the price of a home may increase from $300,000 to $330,000. If the first home buyer has a 10 per cent deposit, the mortgage is $297,000, and is $29,700 higher than it would have been without GST. The FHOG does not offset the GST, as mentioned above. Moreover, the first home owner will repay triple the amount borrowed over the life of the mortgage, so will pay $89,100 more over the life of the mortgage.

The effect of the FHOG was to increase the price of home by multiples of the amount of the grant. Suppose the FHOG was $10,000 at one time in the state of New South Wales. Buyers rushed in to take advantage of the causing the price of homes to increase by $20,000. So the grant gives $10,000 on the one hand but takes $20,000 on the other leading to a net loss for the buyer of $10,000. Moreover, over the life of a mortgage,

---

[32] Source: http://www.firsthome.gov.au/

the homeowner pays triple the amount borrowed so would repay $60,000 more. Subtract the $10,000 grant and the homeowner is $50,000 worse off over the life of the mortgage.

The rationalisation for the FHOG makes no sense, and the FHOG itself led to higher home prices and higher mortgages.

Banks received higher interest payments both as a result of the GST-fuelled increase in mortgages, and the FHOG-fuelled increase in mortgages.

If government cannot 'model' the effects of a financial incentive to purchase, then what can they do? On the one hand they say that they should not interfere in the free market. On the other hand, they justify interfering from time-to-time, but do not understand the impact of interfering. Alternatively, they did understand the impact and intentionally caused higher prices to maintain the bubble. Either way, home buyers have been enslaved for decades longer and banks have been given a gift. This is true whether or not there is a property bubble.

While the grant has been abolished, in large part, the damage has been done and there is no effort underway to reverse the impact.

9. Regulators, policymakers and politicians – a quiet life

APRA and ASIC stick to their mandates. APRA just wants to ensure the banks survive and the interests of people is not on their radar, nor is it likely to be without a cultural and legislative change, or a direction from the Treasurer.

Note also that APRA regards itself as the local office of the Bank of International Settlements ('BIS') in Basel. The BIS itself is known in regulatory and banking circles as just 'Basel'. Basel has no concern about domestic interests or the general welfare of national citizens, but takes a top-down view of the global banking system. As a result, APRA's concern for domestic interests is constrained by its own view of its mandate and by the primacy that APRA gives to Basel. The current APRA chairperson holds key positions on various Basel committees, APRA sends high-performing staff to Basel on secondment which acts as a financial reward, and the previous APRA chairperson did consulting work for Basel after ending his tenure as APRA chairperson. As a result, Basel dictates what APRA does by media release, and sets APRA's priorities. The current APRA chairperson stridently defends this state of affairs.[33] The result is that APRA is not a reliable defender of national interests, and APRA does not even regard its own role as addressing major distortions or illegality in operations connected with the Australian property market, despite the evidence of prudential risk for mortgage lenders.

---

[33] See speech 'International standards and national interests' to the American Chamber of Commerce in Australia Business Briefing in Sydney on 28 June 2017 http://www.apra.gov.au/Speeches/Pages/International-standards-and-national-interests.aspx

ASIC looks for illegality and typically has to be prepared to fight banks in court but where the laws are lax and ASIC's resources are inadequate, ASIC is restricted. Nevertheless, ASIC is soft and accommodating with the large institutions which it regulates,[34,35,36] choosing to take heavy-handed actions on the smaller financial services providers particularly single person operations.[37]

ASIC gives itself an easy life by prosecuting few crimes and ignoring complaints from the public who are at the coalface of bank behaviour. APRA gives itself an easy life by defining its job as implementing international standards such as Basel, and therefore allows its gaze to be directed away from Australia's 'narrow domestic interests' and towards 'international standards'.[38] In this way, APRA does not have to deal with

---

[34] See the submission by Banking and Finance Consumers Support Association to the Senate inquiry into Penalties for white collar crime http://www.aph.gov.au/DocumentStore.ashx?id=be84b97d-5d0a-41d4-acd7-d20fc6db345b&subId=411906

[35] 'How CBA, Westpac, AMP won ASIC spin war' 19 April 2017 *The Australian* Ben Butler http://www.theaustralian.com.au/business/news/how-anz-cba-westpac-amp-won-asic-spin-war/news-story/a9f8e0f631af0e1329810a8b509a5a11

[36] Enforceable undertakings against larger institutions http://www.asic.gov.au/about-asic/asic-investigations-and-enforcement/about-the-enforceable-undertakings-register/

[37] See the ASIC website here for infringement notices which primarily are against small businesses http://www.asic.gov.au/about-asic/asic-investigations-and-enforcement/infringement-notices/

[38] See the political speech by APRA Chairperson to the American Chamber of Commerce in Australia on 28 June 2017 http://www.apra.gov.au/Speeches/Pages/International-standards-and-national-interests.aspx 'Although the political and economic debate in some parts of the world today seems increasingly dominated by narrow domestic interests, and a disregard for broader global perspectives, it is important we do not lose sight of the benefits that international trade and engagement brings all of us.'

messy complications like the systemic instability of the Australian financial system caused by domestic reality of the Australian property market and an Australian financial system run wild.

ASIC and APRA's ideology is, 'Let the market decide.' Who are we to interfere? Adam Smith's fraudulent dicta allowed the British Empire to crush their colonies' manufacturing industries, and today ensure that Western nation states choose to allow the economically powerful, primarily banks, control economies and nations.

10. Misallocation of resources

If governments are so keen on orthodox economics, why have they not considered the 'opportunity cost' – a concept from high school economics – of the overemphasis on residential real estate?

What is the opportunity cost?

Investment, attention and millions of human lives have been consumed in one single pursuit – residential home building and ownership – to the exclusion of capital goods production, science, culture, and nearly every other human endeavour.

Want to know *one of* the factors keeping Australians from achieving on the world stage? Look here.

In May 2015, the *Australian Financial Review* (AFR) announced that property is now Australia's biggest industry:[39]

> Property is now larger than mining, home ownership, or financial services, having almost doubled its contribution to Australian gross domestic product in the last decade.
>
> The industry, including property-related financial, professional and construction services, contributed $182.5 billion to the economy last financial year – 11.5 per cent of GDP – compared with the $147.1 billion value of home ownership and the $140.9 billion mining industry, according to research commissioned for the Property Council of Australia by consultancy AEC Group.
>
> Lobby group the Property Council wants to use the muscle of an industry that directly employs 1.1 million people – making it the

---

[39] Source: http://www.afr.com/real-estate/commercial/property-now-australias-biggest-industry-property-council-says-20150527-ghajmt

second-largest employer after healthcare and social assistance – to
lobby for reforms that would speed up its growth.

The AFR did not consider the opportunity cost. Although the
AFR positions itself as being astute on economic matters, in
fact the AFR is really a promoter of economically
unproductive policy. For the AFR, productivity means lower
wages and longer working hours for the same pay – in effect,
more slave labour – rather than capital investment in
infrastructure, science and manufacturing. The AFR did,
however, quote the Property Council lobby group chief
executive Ken Morrison as saying:

> Our economy needs the property industry to do well, particularly
> as we transition from the mining investment boom.

which, in effect, means that the economy has gone from bad to
worse. The Australian Labor Party (ALP) governments in the
1980s abandoned the ALP's nation-building roots and adopted
the advice of investment bankers to dismantle manufacturing,
adopt free trade, float the currency and become a resource
based economy, in effect, a quarry pit. The AFR notes that we
now are in a property debt slave economy, and quotes the CEO
of a property lobby group admitting this.